The Little Book of Bums

Michael O'Mara Humour

First published in Great Britain in 2000 by
Michael O'Mara Books Limited
9 Lion Yard
Tremadoc Road
London SW4 7NQ

A CIP catalogue record for this book is available from the British Library

ISBN 1-85479-561-9

3 5 7 9 1 0 8 6 4 2

Edited by Andy Armitage

Designed and typeset by Design 23

Made and printed in Great Britain by William Clowes, Beccles, Suffolk.

Bless thee, Bottom! bless thee! thou art translated
WILLIAM SHAKESPEARE,
A Midsummer Night's Dream

Being English I always laugh at anything to do with the lavatory or bottoms
ELIZABETH HURLEY,
quoted in a feature in the Airtours in-flight magazine, January 2000

Introducing the bum

Bum is not quite a four-letter word. Having only three letters, it is allowed – these days at least – to be part of our everyday conversation. Even in polite company, bum can be said without embarrassment, and the word has in the past few years even crept into product terminology, as in bumbag.

Bum is used not only in the anatomical sense, but can describe people – both as noun and adjective – and used as a verb there are several ways to bum.

There are also many words meaning bum, some polite, some downright rude, some only slightly rude and often rather amusing.

In this potpourri of words, sayings, catchphrases, quotations, jokes, we'll look not only at bums but bottoms, posteriors and ... ahem, arses. We hope you don't feel you've got a bum deal.

DRUMMING MUSIC

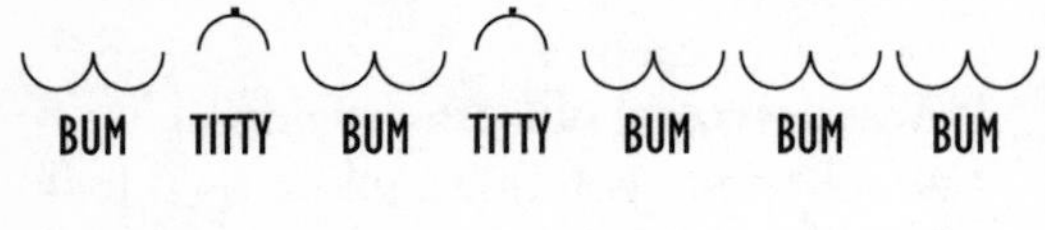

School joke, 1960s

Bum in parts of speech

Bum as a noun

Bum is a noun. It's your backside, your sit-upon, your posterior ... But more euphemisms and synonyms later.

Bum also means – mainly to North Americans – an idler, a loafer, a vagrant. This gives rise to its use as a verb, as we'll see. It was probably a back-formation from *bummer*. It's also a child's word for drink, used as early as 1598.

The Concise Oxford Dictionary says the word that means backside is from late

Middle English but of unknown origin. However, we have better luck with *arse*: *Merriam-Webster's Collegiate Dictionary* of (mainly) American English says, after the headword and part of speech, '[ME *ars*, *ers*, fr. OE *aers*, *ears*; akin to OHG & ON *ars* buttocks, Gk *orrhos* buttocks, *oura* tail]'. So it's from Old English, through Old High German and Old Norse and goes back to the Greeks. Well, it would, wouldn't it?

Bum as a verb

Bum is quite versatile as a verb, too. Apart from describing anal intercourse, it's used for cadging something (*He bummed a ciggie off his mates*).

You can also *bum* a lift when you hitchhike.

You *bum around* when you're being a vagrant, or just loafing or idling.

Bum as an adjective or modifier

Bum comes up in phrases such as *bum's rush*, *bum rap*, *bumfodder*, and *on the bum* (see the section on 'Devastating definitions' below).

Devastating definitions

These definitions culled from various dictionaries and anecdotal sources show the varied use not only of *bum* but its synonyms too (and not all of them refer to your botty).

arse about or around: play the fool; act ungainfully through neglect or stupidity.

arse about face: all wrong; the wrong way round (*That's no good: you've got it all arse about face*).

arse backwards: same as *arse about face*.

arse on backwards: drunk.

arse-cooler: a bustle or dress-improver; refers to the way the old article of feminine attire kept the dress from sticking to the lady's bum. (Also called a bird cage.)

arseholes!: an exclamation to say that something's absurd, to tell someone not to be absurd, or simply to express frustration. Also used as a term of abuse, akin to 'bastards!' or 'cretins!'.

arse-licker or ass-licker: one who acts obsequiously, usually with superiors and for gain. (See also *kiss ass*.)

arse over tip (*or* **arse over tit, a. over t., arse over appetite**): head over heels, but not applied to falling in love (*He fell arse over tip*).

arsy-varsy (*or* **arsy-versy**): topsy-turvy or head over heels.

beach bum, ski bum (etc.): one who devotes a large amount of time to a hobby.

bum freezer: a short jacket.

bum cage: another term for the Victorian bustle.

bum note: wrong note in music.

bum rap: a North American usage, meaning imprisonment on jumped-up charges.

bum rolls: padded rolls worn on the hips under women's dresses in the sixteenth and seventeenth centuries (also called **bearers**; in the eighteenth century they were called **cork rumps** – but simply **dress improvers** in Victorian times).

bum steer: false information.

bumbag: peculiarly British term for a small bag for carrying small items such as money, worn on a belt around the waist or hips. An older slang term, **bum bag** (two words), meant trousers.

bum-bailiff (*or* **bum-baily**)**:** a bailiff with the authority to collect debts and arrest debtors. This *is* connected with backsides, in that it's a historical term, thought to originate from the idea of approaching from behind. These officers were frequently referred to as bums. The French called them *pousse-cul*, meaning push-bum.

bumboat: originally a scavenger's boat removing refuse from ships (also called a dirt boat); later used to describe a small boat that takes provisions to ships. From the Dutch *bumboot*, a broad-beamed fishing boat.

bumf: a colloquial, mainly British, expression used to describe papers and documents – usually mind-numbingly boring stuff you'd rather not have to read. Comes from *bumfodder*. Sometimes spelled *bumph*.

bum fluff: light downy hair on an adolescent's face.

bumfodder: toilet paper; hence *bumf* (preceding).

bummer: a bit like *bum* really, used to mean an idler. Also used to describe some misfortune (*It's a right bummer; That's a bummer of a deal*).

bums on seats: the audience at, e.g., a cinema or theatre, seen as a source of income.

bum's rush: an abrupt dismissal (*She was given the bum's rush*) or a forcible ejection from somewhere.

bust one's ass: try very hard to do something.

buttock lines: longitudinal lines or curves drawn on a plan of a ship to show its fore and aft sections at various distances from the centre line.

candy-ass (N. American): a timid, despicable or cowardly person.

Cherry Bums: an old term for the 11th (Prince of Wales's Own) Hussars. While the word is a corruption of *cherubim*, there's a clear reference to the scarlet trousers that were worn by these soldiers. Another derivation, usually offered by rival cavalry regiments, is that the name comes from an incident during the Peninsular War, when a squadron of the regiment was surrounded and captured by the French in a cherry orchard.

chew (someone's) ass: reprimand severely.

drag (*or* **move, tear** *or* **haul) ass:** hurry or move fast (*We gotta haul ass outta here*).

duck's arse (*or* **ass**) (often called a DA): man's (mainly 1950s) hairstyle, in which the hair is slicked back on both sides and tapered at the nape.

get your ass in (*or* **into**) **gear**: hurry (*If you get your ass in gear, you'll make it*).

half-arsed (*or* assed): incompetent; inadequate.

hard-ass: uncompromising, tough, unyielding person; *hard-assed.*

horse's ass: a stupid person.

kick ass (*or* arse): urge on.

kiss ass: act obsequiously, usually to gain favour.

kiss my arse (*or* **ass**)**, (you can)**: usually said to mean *Not on your life, I'm not doing that; I don't give a monkey's (She can kiss my arse for all I care).*

not give a rat's arse (*or* **ass**)**:** not care at all about something.

on the bum: being a vagrant, loafing around.

pain in the arse (*or* **ass**)**:** someone or something that's an annoyance.

put (*or* **have**) **someone's ass in a sling:** get someone in trouble.

raggedy-arsed (*or* **assed**)**:** shabby, inadequate.

tight-ass (mainly N. American): an inhibited or very conventional person.

whip (*or* bust) someone's ass: use physical force to beat someone in a fight.

you bet your (sweet) ass: you can be very sure (*You can bet your ass he'll beat you every time*).

In other words ... some of bum's synonyms

ampersand
ars musica (play on words, referring to the bum as a noisy vent)
ass (N. American)
blind cheeks
blind Cupid
une boîte aux ordures (French: a box of rubbish, filth)
un borgne (French: one-eyed person)
botty
bumper kit
buns (N. American: the buttocks)
butt

buttocks (from the Old English *buttuc*, probably from the base of *butt*, plus *-ock*)
Daily Mail (rhyming slang – tail)
cakse
can
corybungo
croup
crupper
un cyclope (French: from *Cyclops*, one-eyed)
le département du bas-Rhin (French: a play on words: department of the Lower Rhine; *rein* means kidney, *les reins* means the back)
la derrière, les fesses (French: the behind, buttocks)

dinger (Australian)
dopey
droddum
dummock
fanny (N. American – which can be a source of embarrassment if used in the UK, where it means something close but quite different)
feak
finger and thumb (rhyming slang – bum)
fundament
glutes (from *gluteus*, any of the three muscles in each buttock)
hunkers
jacksy
kazoo

keechters (Scots)
Khyber Pass (rhyming slang – arse/ass)
monocular eyeglass
nock (a notch)
North Pole (rhyming slang – arsehole/asshole)
panier aux crottes (French: basket of dung, or droppings)
peaches
pope's or parson's nose (of a bird's rump)
quoit (Australian)
rearview
la rose des vents (French: rose of winds)
round mouth
rusty-dusty
sit-me-down/sit-upon

le soufflet (French: bellows)
squatter
stern
sweetcakes
tail
tooshie
tuches
tushie (Yiddish)
two fat cheeks and ne'er a nose
le visage sans nez (French: the face
without a nose)
windmill

Bumoticons

There's an Internet convention called emoticons (from *emotion* and *icon*), such as :–) to represent a smile (that one's called a smiley). Several websites have a list of what they call 'ass cons': American, of course.

(_!_) a regular ass

(__!__) a fat ass

(!) a tight ass

(_._) a flat ass

(_*_) a sore ass

(_!__) a lop-sided ass

{_!_} a swishy ass

(_o_) an ass that's been around

(_O_) an ass that's been around
even more

(_x_) kiss my ass

(_X_) leave my ass alone

(_zzz_) a tired ass

(_13_) an unlucky ass

(_$_) money coming out of his ass

(_?_) dumb ass

Bums are ...

beaut
builder's (when bum cleavage is visible above a building worker's low-slung trouser top)
dinky
magic
neat
pert
teensie-weensie
whopping
yer actual
groovy
mean
pear-shaped
rad (radical)
tight/tight little
wicked

Bums aren't (or shouldn't be) ...

bloody
cellulitey
crap
dirty great
flabby
sodding
steaming great
thundering

Quotable quotes: bum in others' mouths

Maugham! He couldn't write bum on a wall; and if he could, he'd spell it Baugham.

(spoken of Robin Maugham, the novelist, by his friend, the playwright Terence Rattigan)

Blow, winds, and crack your cheeks! rage! blow!

WILLIAM SHAKESPEARE,
King Lear

Nineteen ninety-nine became the year of my bottom.

The TV star GAIL PORTER, whose nude image was projected on to the Houses of Parliament

Derk was the nyght as pich, or as the cole,
And at the wyndow out she putte hir hole,
And Absolon, hym fil no bet be wers,
But with his mouth he kiste hir naked ers
Ful savourly, er he were war of this.
Abak he stirte, and thoughte it was amys,
For wel he wiste a womman hath no berd.
He felte a thyng al rough and long yherd,
And seyde, 'Fy! allas! what have I to do?'
'Tehee!' quod she, and clapte the wyndow to.

GEOFFREY CHAUCER, *The Canterbury Tales*,
'The Miller's Tale'

Jesus loves you ... everyone else thinks you're an ahole.**

BUMPER STICKER, USA.

When shit becomes valuable, the poor will be born without assholes.

HENRY MILLER, US novelist

Never assume, for it makes an ASS out of U and ME.

ANON.

The cocktail party ... was originally invented by dogs. They are simply bottom-sniffings raised to the rank of formal ceremonies.

LAWRENCE DURRELL

The place where honour's lodg'd,
As wise philosophers have judged;
Because a kick in that part more
Hurts honour than deep wounds sore.

SAMUEL BUTLER, *Hudibras*

Mr Dedalus, staring from the empty fireplace at Ned Lambert's quizzing face, asked of it sourly:

- Agonizing Christ, wouldn't it give you a heartburn on your arse?

JAMES JOYCE, *Ulysses*

Ars Musica: a bum fiddle
The 1881 Dictionary of the Vulgar Tongue

Bum Brusher: schoolmaster
IBID.

Buttock Ball: the amorous congress
IBID.

Buttock and File: a common whore and a pickpocket
IBID.

Buttock and Twang, or Down Buttock and Sham File: a common whore but no pickpocket

IBID.

Buttock and Tongue: a scolding wife

IBID.

Buttocking Shop: a brothel

IBID.

Your breeches sit close enough to your bum.

BEN JONSON, *Bartholomew Fair*

And first his bum you see him clap
Upon the Queen of Sheba's lap.

JONATHAN SWIFT, *Intelligencer*

'Tha's got such a nice tail on thee,' he said, in the throaty caressive dialect. 'Tha's got the nicest arse of anybody. It's the nicest, nicest woman's arse as is! An' ivery bit of it is woman, woman sure as nuts. Tha'rt not one o' them button-arsed lasses as should be lads, are ter! Tha's got a real soft sloping bottom on thee, as a man loves in 'is guts. It's a bottom as could hold the world up, it is!'

D. H. LAWRENCE, *Lady Chatterley's Lover*

ESCALUS: Well, no more of it,
Master Froth: farewell.

Exit FROTH

Come you hither to me, Master
tapster. What's your name, Master
tapster?
POMPEY: Pompey.
ESCALUS: What else?
POMPEY: Bum, sir.
ESCALUS: Troth, and your bum is
the greatest thing about you; so that in
the beastliest sense you are Pompey
the Great.

WILLIAM SHAKESPEARE,
Measure for Measure

If you voted for Clinton in the last election, you can't take a dump here. Your asshole is in Washington.

GRAFFITO in the men's room at the Outback Steakhouse, Tacoma, Washington

Hail Matrimony, made of Love!
To thy wide gates how great a drove
On purpose to be yok'd do come;
Widows and Maids and Youths also,
That lightly trip on beauty's toe,
Or sit on beauty's bum.

WILLIAM BLAKE,
'Songs From an Island in the Moon'

That lazy bum-delighting thing, Ridly the Chancellor.

JOHN WOLCOT,
Lyric Odes to the Royal Academicians

Sir Thomas Malory tells in his great work *Le Morte d'Arthur* (c. 1450-c. 1469) of the adventures of Sir Lancelot (Launcelot), among others. But poor Sir L got more than he bargained for when dozing by the water's edge. Because there was 'a lady that dwelled in that foreyste, and she was a grete hunteresse', and she was out hunting deer.

She happened upon the deer, a hind, and 'put a brode arow in her bowe and shot at the hynde, and so she overshotte the hynde, and so by myssefortune the arow smote sir Launcelot in the thycke of the buttok ...'

After Lancelot has berated her and there's a short exchange ('"Alas," sayde sir Launcelot, "ye have myscheved me"'), he 'pulled oute the arow and leffte the hede stylle in hys buttok, and so he wente waykely unto the ermytayge, evermore bledynge as he went'.

Having been well and truly lanced a lot, Sir L gets to the hermitage (the'ermytayge'), and the hermit (the 'ermyte') 'gate oute the arow-hede oute of sir Launcelottis buttoke, and muche of hys bloode he shed; and the wounde was passynge sore and unhappyly smytten, for hit was on such a place that he myght nat sytte in no sadyll'.

SIR THOMAS MALORY, *Le Morte d'Arthur*,
Book XVIII: *Launcelot and Guinevere*

Patriot women take their hazel wands, and fustigate [beat] ... broad bottom of priests.

THOMAS CARLYLE, *French Revolution*

Cantwell had answered: Go and fight your match. Give Cecil Thunder a belt. I'd like to see you. He'd give you a toe in the rump for yourself. That was not a nice expression.

JAMES JOYCE, *Ulysses*

The well-known journalist and politician Horatio Bottomley had called on a certain Lord Cholmondeley (pronounced Chumley), and, when the butler opened the door in answer to this ring, enquired whether Lord Cholmondeley was at home. He pronounced the name exactly as it is spelt, and the butler, seeking to correct him, replied that Lord 'Chumley' was home.

'Good,' replied Bottomley. 'Tell him that Horatio Bumley would like a word with him.'

KENNETH EDWARDS, *I Wish I'd Said That! A collection of witty replies*

Arrah, sit down on the parliamentary side of your arse for Christ' sake and don't be making a public exhibition of yourself.

JAMES JOYCE, *Ulysses*

Supposin', supposin'
My bum was a-closin'
An' you 'ad your nose in,
Supposin', supposin'.

MY AUNTIE LUCY when a girl (who in adult life denied all authorship!)

I test my bath before I sit,
And I'm always moved to wonderment
That what chills the finger not a bit
Is so frigid upon the fundament.

OGDEN NASH, 'Samson Agonistes'

a politician is an arse upon
which everyone has sat
except a man

e. e. cummings, *1 x 1*, No. 10

Sure, deck your lower limbs in pants;
Yours are the limbs, my sweeting.
You look divine as you advance -
Have you seen yourself retreating?

OGDEN NASH, 'What's the Use?'

Beauty for some provides escape,
Who gain a happiness in eyeing
The gorgeous buttocks of the ape
Or autumn sunsets exquisitely dying.

ALDOUS HUXLEY, 'The Ninth Philosopher's Song'

...It's no go the Government grants, it's no go the elections,
Sit on your arse for fifty years and hang your hat on a pension.

LOUIS MACNEICE, 'Bagpipe Music'

Grip your gun like a man, brother!
Let's have a crack at Holy Russia,
Mother
Russia
With her big, fat arse!
Freedom, freedom! Down with the Cross!

ALEKSANDR BLOK, 'The Twelve'

This English woman is so refined
She has no bosom and no behind.

STEVIE SMITH, 'This Englishwoman'

I don't want loyalty. I want *loyalty*. I want him to kiss my ass in Macy's window at high noon and tell me it smells of roses. I want his pecker in my pocket.

US President LYNDON BAINES JOHNSON, of a potential aide, quoted in David Halberstam, *The Best and the Brightest*

A real Centaur – part man, part horse's ass.

DEAN ACHESON, of President Lyndon Baines Johnson, letter, 13 April 1968

Boys do now cry 'Kiss my Parliament!' instead of 'Kiss my arse!' so great and general a contempt is the Rump come to among all men, good and bad.

SAMUEL PEPYS, of the Rump Parliament, diary entry, 7 February 1670

Writing and travel broaden your ass if not your mind and I like to write standing up.

ERNEST HEMINGWAY, letter, 9 July 1950

Cover your ass – the bureaucrat's method of protecting his posterior from posterity.

WILLIAM SAFIRE, *Safire's Political Dictionary*

People ask why I ride with my bottom in the air. Well, I've got to put it somewhere.

Lester Piggott, quoted in Colin Jarman (ed.), *The Guinness Dictionary of Sports Quotations*

Every man also has his moral backside which he refrains from showing unless he has to and keeps covered as long as possible with the trousers of decorum.
Georg Christoph Lichtenberg, *Aphorisms*

Two buttocks of one bum.
T. STURGE MOORE, of Hilaire Belloc and G. K. Chesterton

Portsmouth, that pocky bitch
A damn'd Papistical drab
An ugly deform'd witch
Eaten up with the mange and scab
This French hag's pocky bum
So powerful is of late
Although it's both blind and dumb
It rules both Church and State.

ANONYMOUS, 'A Satire', of Louise de Kéroualle, who was one of Charles II's mistresses, and whom he created Duchess of Portsmouth

He kissed the plump mellow yellor smellor melons of her rump, on each plump melonous hemisphere, in their mellow yellow furrow, with obscure prolonged provocative mellonsmellonous osculation.

JAMES JOYCE, *Finnegans Wake*

You can shake
Just like it would a tree
The way you shake it
It's pleasing me
Just let me tell you
A thing or two
A plenty of people shake it
But not like you

ANNA BELL, 'Shake It, Black Bottom'

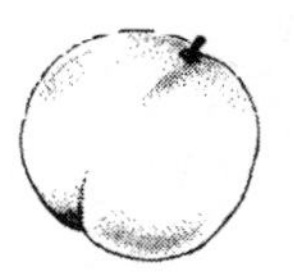

DAVID GARRICK, having received an account from Berry Brothers, the St James's wine merchants, wrote a furious quatrain by way of answer, which began:

I have received your Bilberry ...

and ended:

I will come and kick your Raspberry

Sciatica: he cur'd it by boiling his buttock.

JOHN AUBREY, *Brief Lives*, 'Sir Jonas Moore'

It is like a barber's chair that fits all buttocks.

WILLIAM SHAKESPEARE, *All's Well That Ends Well*

There's a boy across the river with a bottom like a peach,
But alas, I cannot swim.

'ZUCHMI DIL', Pathan warrior's song from the North-West Frontier area of the India-Afghanistan (now Pakistan-Afghanistan) border

...And their behinds
Cause th' astonish'd nightingale to sing.

JAMES ELROY FLECKER, suppressed verse from 'Hassan'

The people's flag is deepest pink,
It's not as red as you might think...
The working class can kiss my arse –
I've got the foreman's job at last.

ANON., parody of James M. Connell's socialist song 'The Red Flag'

The sun like a bishop's bottom,
Rosy and round and hot,
Rose up as down we shot 'em,
As down upon 'em we shot.

RAYMOND ASQUITH, parody of Rudyard Kipling's verse

On solemn asses fall plush sinecures,
So keep a straight face and sit tight on yours.

X. J. KENNEDY, 'To a Young Poet'

Higgledy-piggledy
Heliogabalus
Lurched through the Forum, his
Bottom a-wag,
Vainly pretending to
Gynaecological
Problems beneath his Im-
Perial drag

JOHN HOLLANDER, 'Heliogabalus'

While you're saving your face you're losing your ass.

US President LYNDON BAINES JOHNSON

Les visages sont si tristes, mais les derrières sont si gaies.
(The faces are so sad, but the bottoms are so jolly.)

FRENCH DIPLOMAT of 'modern' dancing in 1918, quoted by Sir Thomas Beecham

The wisest aunt, telling the saddest tale,
Sometime for three-foot stool mistaketh me;
Then slip I from her bum, down topples she,
And 'tailor' cries, and falls into a cough;
And then the whole quire hold their hips and loff.

WILLIAM SHAKESPEARE, *A Midsummer Night's Dream*

I do not care what a dogs pedigree may be ... millionaires and bums taste about alike to me.

DON MARQUIS, *archy and mehitabel*

Boys don't make passes at female smart-asses.

LETTY COTTIN POGREBIN, US journalist and writer, echoing Dorothy Parker's famous 1937 lines, Men seldom make passes/At girls who wear glasses

He hasn't got enough sense to bore assholes in wooden hobbyhorses.

DOROTHY PARKER, of a notoriously stupid Hollywood producer

The only thing this actress offers us in the way of change is the constant covering up and uncovering of her charming derrière.

JUDITH CRIST on Brigitte Bardot

Frenchmen resemble apes, who, climbing up a tree from branch to branch, never cease going till they come to the highest branch, and there show their bare behinds.

MICHEL EYQUEM DE MONTAIGNE

The plastic asshole of the world.

WILLIAM FAULKNER, on Los Angeles

Wenn ich sitze, will ich nicht
sitzen, wie mein Sitz-Fleischmöchte
sondern wie mein Sits-Geistsich
säsze er, den Stuhl sich flöchte.

(When I sit I don't like to
sit the way my fleshy bottom wants to,
but in the way that my spiritual
bottom would, if I sat,
intertwine itself with the chair.)

CHRISTIAN MORGANSTERN, 'Der
Aesthet', from *Der Gingganz*

They can kiss my rear end, if they can leap that high.
PETE WILSON, Governor of California, about Democrat critics of his proposals to reform the law on illegal immigrants

During the filming of *Lifeboat* (1944), Mary Anderson, one of the actresses who starred in it, asked the director, **'Mr Hitchcock, which do you think is my best side?'**
She received the reply, **'My dear, you're sitting on it.'**

You can park a bike on that bum.
ANON.

I'm that hungry I could eat a baby's bum through the back of a cane chair.

IBID.

Her arse wobbles like two boys fighting under a blanket/like two ferrets fighting in a sack.

IBID.

Sayings about bums

As close as God's curse to a whore's arse (*or* As close as shirt and shitten arse).

Early nineteenth-century saying.

Beer, bum and bacca.

A reference, since about 1870, to the pleasures of a sailor's life (though a later variant gives *rum, bum and bacca*); George Melly's autobiography *Rum, Bum and Concertina* dealt with his life in the navy.

Bum to bum.

Meaning no sex tonight.

Cover your ass.

US saying, originating during the Vietnam War before becoming a general catchphrase for ensuring you're not vulnerable.

Don't get your arse in an uproar.

Twentieth-century saying, with US equivalents substituting *balls* or *bowels* for *arse*.

Don't let your mouth overload your ass.

Saying from the Los Angeles black ghetto, meaning don't talk too much.

Don't tear the arse out of it!

A mid-twentieth-century army saying, meaning don't exaggerate or don't put too much effort into it.

Hasn't got a sixpence to scratch his arse with (*or* Hasn't got a ha'penny to jingle on a tombstone).

Used from nineteenth to mid-twentieth centuries – the former being the later, and perhaps indicating the rise in the cost of living.

He couldn't find his arse with both hands.

Twentieth-century expression to mean that someone is drunk, nowadays often also used to mean that a person is stupid.

He couldn't hit a bull in the arse with a scoop-shovel.

Twentieth-century Canadian saying, referring to a bad marksman (the polite version of this substitutes a barn door or the inside of a barn for a bull's arse).

He doesn't know his ass from a hole in the ground (*or* ... from third base *or* ... from a hot rock *or* ... from his elbow).

Twentieth-century US saying.

He has his ass in a sling.

Used in the US since World War Two – referring to someone so deep in trouble that it's as though he had his ass (or arse) kicked so hard that he needs a sling to support it.

He'd lend his arse and shite through his ribs.

Quoted in Francis Grose, *A Classical Dictionary of the Vulgar Tongue*, 1785; refers to someone being silly with his money.

He'd lose his arse if it was loose.

In use about 1770 to 1860. Quoted in Francis Grose, *A Classical Dictionary of the Vulgar Tongue*, 1785; a more modern equivalent is *He'd lose his head if it wasn't screwed on*.

Here's me head, me arse is comin'.

Late nineteenth century, referring to a woman in high heels, making her walk with head and shoulders well forward and bum bringing up the rear.

If I stick a broom up my arse I can sweep the hangar at the same time.

RAF saying, from the 1920s, meaning I've got too much to do; there are variations on the same theme.

It fits him like a duck's ass.

Used in the US since about 1920 and referring to clothing that's too tight; variations include *Tight as a duck's arse* for mean with money (sometimes with '*and that's waterproof*' added).

It's bad manners to speak when your arse is full.

Twentieth century, said to someone who farts noisily in public; echoes the adage that you shouldn't speak with a full mouth.

Like a thimble on a bull's arse.

Twentieth-century Northern and/or rural saying for a small cap on a large head.

Like flies around a bull's arse.

North-Country saying since the late nineteenth century, echoing the equally graphic *Like flies around a honey [or jam] pot.*

Living on the bone of his arse.

Australian saying indicating extreme poverty.

My arse is dragging.

Canadian saying since about 1915 meaning I'm knackered.

Shake the lead out of your ass.

US and Canadian saying, meaning get a move on, or move ass!

She had a hair across her arse (or ass).

Canadian expression indicating that the person in question was irritable.

She walks like she's got a feather up her ass.

Twentieth-century Canadian saying, of a woman with a mincing gait.

The Persian Gulf's the arsehole of the world, and Sha'aiba's halfway up it.

Army and RAF saying, originating in the 1920s, when Britain's policy of 'imperial policing' saw servicemen stationed in Iraq.

Aye, my arse and thy face.

Yorkshire insult, said in response to the request 'Have you got a match?'

Took his arse in his hands and left.

Twentieth-century saying indicating someone making a would-be dignified exit

A wet arse and no fish.

Nineteenth to twentieth-century saying that began among trawlermen or anglers indicating a fruitless errand

You couldn't see his arse for dust.

Saying dating back to the late nineteenth century, said of a hasty departure, and echoing a song from the musical *The White Horse Inn* with the words, 'You won't see my heels for the dust'.

You think you've got the lights of Piccadilly Circus shining out of your arsehole.

British saying dating back to about 1900 and used mostly by the armed services; more familiar these days as *He thinks the sun shines out of his arse.*

You want to know all the ins and outs of a nag's arse.

Cockney, late nineteenth to early twentieth century, said to an inquisitive person.

Your asshole's sucking wind.

A Canadian expression common in World War Two, meaning you don't know what you're talking about.

Bum search

Find books on 'bum' at barnesandnoble.com

Buy and sell 'bum' and millions of other items at eBay

Find an expert on 'bum' at EXP.com

Shopping: shop for 'bum' or related products.

Result of an Internet search on 'bum' for the compiling of this book!

Other 'Little Book' titles published by
Michael O'Mara Books Ltd:

The Little Book of Farting – ISBN 1-85479-445-0
The Little Book of Stupid Men – ISBN 1-85479-454-X
The Little Toilet Book – ISBN 1-85479- 456-6
The Little Book of Venom – ISBN 1-85479-446-9
The Little Book of Pants – ISBN 1-85479-477-9
The Little Book of Pants 2 – ISBN 1-85479-557-0
The Little Book of Revenge – ISBN 1-85479-562-7
The Little Book of Voodoo – ISBN 1-85479-560-0
The Little Book of Blondes – ISBN 1-85479-558-9
The Little Book of Magical Love Spells –
ISBN 1-85479-559-7

If you would like more information, please contact our UK
Sales Department:

fax: 020 7 622 6956
e-mail: jokes@michaelomarabooks.com